D0100375

BASEBALL ·TIPS·

BASEBALL ·TIPS·

by **DEAN HUGHES** and **TOM HUGHES**

illustrated by **DENNIS LYALL**

RANDOM HOUSE 🏠 NEW YORK

Text copyright © 1993 by Dean Hughes and Tom Hughes.
Illustrations copyright © 1993 by Dennis Lyall. All rights
reserved under International and Pan-American Copyright
Conventions. Published in the United States by Random House,
Inc., New York, and simultaneously in Canada by Random House
of Canada Limited, Toronto.

Library of Congress Cataloging-in-Publication Data

Hughes, Dean

Baseball tips / by Dean Hughes and Tom Hughes ; illustrated by
Dennis Lyall.

p.   cm.

Summary: A beginner's guide to baseball basics with tips on how to
hit, run bases, field, throw, and sharpen skills through practice.

ISBN 0-679-83642-X (trade)   0-679-93642-4 (lib. bdg.)

1. Baseball—Juvenile literature.   [1. Baseball.]   I. Hughes,
Tom.   II. Lyall, Dennis, ill.   III. Title.

GV867.5.H84   1993

796.357—dc20   92-13406

Manufactured in the United States of America

10   9   8   7   6   5   4   3   2

CONTENTS

PART FOUR

ATTITUDE

INTRODUCTION

Baseball is a great game.

There's nothing like being at the park on a hot summer afternoon: the bases loaded and you're up.

The infielders are all shouting, "Hey, batta, batta, batta." And someone on the bench yells, "Hey, kid, you can't hit!"

Then the pitcher fires a fastball down the middle.

Crack!

You connect! A line drive—straight as a rope—shoots past the infield and lands for a base hit.

You dig for first. One run, two runs score.

What a feeling!

You won't get a hit every time up. You won't field every grounder cleanly either—no one does. But this book can teach you what you need to know to play the game well—fielding, catching, hitting, throwing, pitching, running the bases.

If you keep things simple, the game isn't so hard. It all comes from knowing how, and *practicing*. To help you out, we've come up with just three basic, easy-to-remember rules for each skill.

Your job is to get out on that field and have a great time!

Special Note Remember, wear a protective helmet whenever you play or practice.

PART ONE

UP TO BAT

1

HITTING

Your bat connects with a fastball.

Crack!

Don't you love that sound—and the feeling that runs up your arms? And what a beautiful sight, when you see the ball jump off your bat and you *know* you've got a base hit!

If you want to get "good wood" on the ball (even if the bat is aluminum), these are the things to do.

THE BIG THREE OF HITTING

1. Keep your eyes on the ball.
2. Take a level swing.
3. Don't swing too hard.

Have you heard this advice already? Is this what your coach tells you? But how—exactly—do you do it? It all begins with the way you stand at the plate, and that's called your "stance."

Stance

The key to a good stance is *balance*.
Here's how you get it:

1. Stand with your feet about
   as far apart as your shoulders.
2. Lean forward just a little,
   and keep your weight
   slightly more on your back
   foot—but don't bend your
   body too far in any direction.
3. Keep your shoulders level.
4. Turn your head toward the
   pitcher far enough that your
   chin touches your shoulder.
5. Hold your bat still and in a
   relaxed position. Keep your
   hands above your waist but
   below your shoulders.

Look at yourself in a mirror. Have you got it? Have someone
give you a little push. Is your balance solid? Good. Now you
are ready to use the "Big Three."

Keep Your Eyes on the Ball

If your head is turned so that it is touching your shoulder, you
can see the ball with *both* eyes. That's important.

Try to spot the ball as early as possible—as soon as it leaves
the pitcher's hand.

Follow the ball all the way to the bat.

Take a Level Swing

Grip the bat with your hands together and your knuckles lined up, but don't squeeze too tight. If you're right-handed, your right hand should be on top. If you're left-handed, your left hand should be on top.

At first, you may want to keep your bottom hand a couple of inches above the knob of the bat. This gives you a little less power, but you'll have more bat control.

Hold your bat in a position that keeps your shoulders level. Now continue to hold your shoulders level as you swing.

A downward swing will chop the ball onto the ground. An upward swing will make it pop up into the air.

As you swing, stride toward the pitcher. Don't step toward the plate or away from it.

Take a smooth stride. Don't hitch your weight back and then forward.

Take a short stride—less than a foot forward. A long stride will cause you to drop your front shoulder and will throw your balance off.

Don't Swing Too Hard

"Don't try to kill the ball!" your coach shouts. But why not? Don't you have to swing hard to hit the ball a long way? No, you don't. Bat speed doesn't come from your shoulders and arms, but from wrist action. Both wrists should be level and loose, not stiff. And they should suddenly *snap* the bat forward just as the bat crosses the plate.

When you swing hard with your arms, your head jerks and you don't see the ball well. Your shoulders get thrown up or down, and you don't take a level swing.

Now that you know *what* to do, you have to practice until you can do it every time.

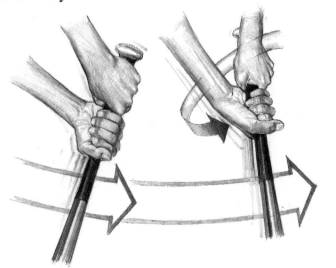

STRIKE ZONE

♦ ♦ ♦ ♦ **P R A C T I C I N G** ♦ ♦ ♦ ♦

When you practice hitting, have the catcher or another player call balls and strikes. Swing only at strikes—hittable pitches in the strike zone.

Bad pitches are hard to hit, so don't swing at them in practice. That can get you into bad habits.

Here's how to practice the ''Big Three'' of hitting:

1. *Keep your eyes on the ball*. Watch ten pitches go by—and *don't swing*. Follow the ball across the plate until your chin bumps your back shoulder.

On the eleventh pitch (if it's a strike), bring the bat to the ball. Swing naturally, not overly hard, and follow the ball right to the bat.

2. *Take a level swing*. Stand in front of a mirror with your bat. Take your stance and see whether your shoulders are level.

If one shoulder is higher than the other, adjust your stance.

Now, swing the bat easily. If a shoulder drops, ask yourself why. Are you dropping the bat before you swing? Are you shifting your weight?

Keep adjusting until you can swing the bat without moving your head or shoulders up and down.

Now try your swing without the mirror. Have a friend watch to be sure your shoulders stay level.

3. *Don't swing too hard*. Practice your swing when no one is pitching. Remind yourself to swing naturally with a good snap of the wrists. Don't force your arm speed.

Be sure to use a bat you can swing easily. A bat that is too heavy will slow down your wrist action.

2

BUNTING

Good baseball players play smart. And sometimes a bunt is a smart play.

You may be playing in a league that doesn't allow bunting. But bunting is an important skill, and you might as well start practicing now. When you move to a more advanced league, you will be ready.

Usually it's your coach who will decide when you should bunt. He or she may want you to bunt in order to move up a runner on the bases—even though you'll probably be out. That's called a "sacrifice" bunt.

Or your coach may have you lay down a bunt so that a runner from third base can score. That's called a "squeeze play."

You can also bunt for a base hit. When fielders are expecting you to blast a long hit, they play farther back. That might be the time for you to drop a bunt down. If you can get on base, a hit that only rolls a few feet is just as good as a line drive!

So what's the trick to bunting right? Try to remember:

THE BIG THREE OF BUNTING

1. Hold your bat correctly.
2. Keep your eyes on the ball.
3. Let the ball hit your bat.

This sounds a little like the "Big Three" of hitting, doesn't it? Well, it should. Bunting is a special kind of hitting.

Let's start with your stance.

Stance

Begin with the balanced stance that you use for hitting.

You then turn so that your body is facing the pitcher. Don't lift your feet. Just twist on your toes while bending your knees a little more than usual.

Move into your bunt stance as late as possible. You don't want to tip off the defense that you are about to bunt.

On the other hand, don't wait so long that you have to hurry. You want to be all set up and balanced when the ball gets to you.

Now use the "Big Three" of bunting.

Hold Your Bat Right

At the same time that you move into the bunting stance:

1. Slide your top hand along the bat to the label. (Keep your fingers *behind* the bat, so they won't get hurt.)
2. Raise the bat chest high, with the bat straight across the front of home plate. Keep the knob of the bat near the middle of your chest.

Keep Your Eyes on the Ball

It is easy to watch the ball when you bunt because you're looking straight at the pitcher.

Spot the ball early and watch it all the way to your bat.

Let the Ball Hit Your Bat

Don't hit the ball. Instead, let the ball hit your bat. And let the bat give just a little. That way the ball won't roll too far.

If you start with the bat chest high, you'll know that a pitch that comes in higher can't be a strike. Don't try to bunt a high pitch, or the ball will pop in the air.

When you see the pitch is going to be a ball, pull the bat back and let the pitch go by. You lose your surprise, but trying to bunt a bad pitch hardly ever works.

If the pitch is in the strike zone, you will probably have to move the bat to make contact. But keep the bat level. If necessary, go down for the pitch by *bending your knees*—not your elbows.

A good bunt should roll about halfway to third base or first base. That way, the in-fielders have to run a long way to get to the ball. Then they have a tough throw to first.

By then you've reached first—with a big grin on your face!

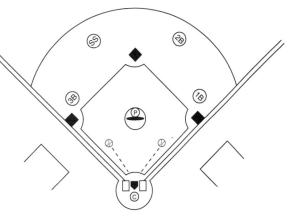

A good bunt should roll halfway to third or first.

1. *Hold your bat correctly*. Practice the toe-twist from a batting stance to a bunting stance. Keep your head and shoulders steady. At the same time, slide your top hand into the proper position. Keep the bat chest high.

Practice until you can change stances smoothly and without losing your balance.

2. *Keep your eyes on the ball*. With your bat in the bunting position, let ten pitches go by. Watch them all the way and decide whether they are strikes—good pitches to bunt. Pull the bat back for now. Concentrate on deciding whether the pitches are in the strike zone.

3. *Let the ball hit your bat*. On the eleventh pitch, move your bat in front of the ball (if it is a strike). Bend your knees, not your elbows, and keep the bat level.

After you have let the ball hit your bat ten times, practice turning from a batting stance to a bunting stance with each pitch. Try to guide the bunt either along the first-base or third-base line.

Now add the last part: When the bunt goes down, take off for first base. And run *hard!*

3

BASE RUNNING

Pow!

You're on first. Your teammate slams a hit right over second base. What do you do now?

Run, of course!

But there's more to base running than . . . just running. You need to know:

```
┌─── THE BIG THREE OF BASE RUNNING ───┐
│                                       │
│        1. Round the bases.            │
│        2. Always run hard.            │
│        3. Be alert.                   │
│                                       │
└───────────────────────────────────────┘
```

Do you know what it means to "round" the bases? Let's talk about it.

Round the Bases

When you run the bases, you don't always run straight from one base to the next. Sometimes you run outside the lines, and sometimes you cut inside.

After you hit the ball, don't drop the bat in the batter's box—but don't give it a long toss, either. Carry it a step or two and then drop it a few feet to the side of the baseline, where it won't be in anyone's way.

As you run to first, run about a foot outside the line. If you are digging hard to beat a throw to first, run straight on through the bag. The rules allow you to do that.

But what if the ball goes through the infield, and you see a chance to go to second? Watch the coach as you approach the bag. Listen for him to tell you whether to head for second or hold up.

If the coach sends you on, round first by looping outside the line a little. Then cut *inside* the bag. Step on the *inside corner* of the bag with your *right* foot.

Or let's say you're on first and your teammate hits a ground ball. You run for second. If you see no chance to go to third, run straight at second.

But what if the ball gets through the infield?

If you run straight at second, you'll find it hard—and slow—to turn toward third. So, after you run about ten feet from first, you begin to angle a little to your right. As you near second, you loop even more to the right and then "round the base."

When you loop outside the baseline, you already have the angle to head toward third. You won't have to slow down to make the turn.

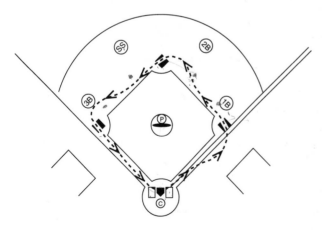

Rounding the bases.

If your coach signals you to go for home, round the base again, and tag third base the same way: *inside corner, right foot.*

Always Run Hard

This might sound too silly to talk about. But it's not. Every team would score more runs if all players ran hard all the time.

You hit a ground ball right to the shortstop. You figure it's a sure out. But it's easy to miss a grounder. And that shortstop has a long throw to make. So run hard and force the shortstop to hurry a little.

Just a little slip, or a poor throw, and you're on base.

Or let's say you knock the ball past the second baseman. It rolls into shallow right field. A single—right?

You trot down to first and stand on the bag.

But what if you run hard and make the turn?

Maybe the right fielder stumbles or lets the ball roll by—or picks up the ball and tosses it to the pitcher without paying attention to you.

If you made it to first quickly, and you go hard to second, you just might turn a single into a double.

Be Alert

Here comes the pitch. The batter swings!

At that moment, lots of things can happen. If you're on base, you have to be ready for anything.

In time, you will learn all the kinds of situations that might come up in a baseball game. You will know what to do. But for now, remember to listen to your coach. And above all, *watch the ball* and be ready to react to whatever happens.

You're on second. On a single, will you stop at third—or try to score? It depends on where the ball is hit, how hard it is hit, and how well the outfielder handles it.

So *watch* the ball as you run, and know what's happening. Then look to your third-base coach. Two hands up means ''stop.'' An arm waving in a big circle means ''keep going.''

Go hard!

But what if you're on second and the batter hits the ball in the air to the outfield? Play it ''halfway,'' by running halfway to third. If the outfielder catches the ball, you go back to second. If the outfielder doesn't make the catch, you run to third and maybe home.

Sometimes the fly ball is hit right to an outfielder. It seems a sure out. That's the time to go back to your base and "tag up." As soon as the outfielder catches the ball, you take off for the next base—if you feel sure you can make it.

1. ***Round the bases.*** Practice running around the bases. You can even combine batting practice with a base-running drill.

Hit the ball, drop the bat out of the way, and then run to first. As you near first, loop outside the baseline a little and run inside the bag. Tag the base with your right foot.

As you head for second, loop outside the baseline again. Tag all the bases the same way.

2. ***Always run hard.***

3. ***Be alert.***

No matter when you play baseball, even if you're only playing with some friends for fun, play the game the same way. Run hard and watch for chances to take an extra base. If you take it easy in practice games, that will become your habit. So play with excitement and concentration every time.

UP TO BAT

4

STEALING AND SLIDING

Most leagues for younger players do not allow stealing or sliding. But you can learn the ideas behind stealing and sliding now. Practice them when your coach thinks the time is right.

The pitcher is winding up. You take off for second base, running *hard*. You slide for the bag just as the shortstop takes the throw. The shortstop slaps down the tag, and for a moment you're not sure.

And then you hear the umpire bellow, *"Saaaa-eeeeeffff!"*

You hop up and wave to the fans. You're a hero.

Maybe.

You took a big chance. What if you had gotten thrown out? Or what if your slide was wrong and you hurt your ankle hitting the bag?

You need to know the right way to steal and slide. Mastering these skills will help you get to the base safe—not out *and* not hurt. So learn:

1. Know where the ball is.
2. Watch the pitcher's knees.
3. Use the ''pop-up'' slide (if you have to slide).

Know Where the Ball Is

A good baseball player *always* knows where the ball is.

When you're on base, the ball becomes your enemy. You don't want to be tagged out simply because you weren't watching.

Don't get caught by the old trick: the first baseman goes over and talks to the pitcher and then walks back—with the ball hidden in his glove. When you step off the base, he tags you!

Stay on base until you know where the ball is *for sure*—even if you're in a league that allows taking a lead. (Taking a lead means taking two or three steps off the base, but it never means getting so far away that the pitcher can throw to the first baseman and tag you out.)

Watch the Pitcher's Knees

Your coach may signal to you to steal, or give you the green light to steal when you see a good chance.

Either way, watch those pitchers. Get to know the timing and motion of each one. Bluff a couple of times and try to draw a throw. You need to know how quick the pitcher is at throwing to first.

Find the earliest moment that you can run. In leagues that don't allow taking a lead, judge the speed of the pitch and the skill of the catcher.

Once you take a lead, learn to watch the pitcher's knees, not his or her arm motion.

A good pitcher can make a throw to first look like a pitch home—if you watch only arms and shoulders. But if you watch where the pitcher's leg goes, you won't be tricked. Once the pitcher strides toward the plate, take off.

And go hard.

Run on a straight line, but after a few steps, glance to see where the ball is. If the catcher throws the ball into center field, you need to see that. Then you can round the base and keep going.

Use the "Pop-Up" Slide
(If You Have to Slide)

The reason a base runner slides is to get down low and avoid a tag. But it's also the fastest way to get to the bag.

Slide if you need to—but stay on your feet when you can. When you're on your feet, you're ready to head for the next base if the throw is bad.

Don't slide headfirst!

Some big leaguers slide headfirst. But it's dangerous. And you can't get back on your feet fast when you're on your stomach.

So use the pop-up slide.

Run straight at the bag. Drop onto one side of the seat of your pants. Stretch with the leg on the other side. But don't lock your knee. Let it give as your foot hits the base.

The other leg should be bent at the knee, with the foot tucked under the stretched-out leg. When you hit the bag with the front foot, your body will pop up partway, and you can use the foot you're "sitting on" to stand up the rest of the way.

And you're ready to run again, if you get the chance.

While sliding, keep your arms out of the way. Make your hands into fists so you don't jam your fingers or catch them on anything.

♦ ♦ ♦ ♦ P R A C T I C I N G ♦ ♦ ♦ ♦

1. *Stealing.* Study pitchers and try to find that crucial instant when you can take off. Get to know all the pitchers in your league.

Try stealing on your own pitchers during team practice. That helps the pitcher and first baseman learn how to keep a base runner close to the base, and it lowers the chance of someone stealing in a game. When you take off, practice running straight at the next bag and taking a quick look for the ball as you run.

2. *Sliding.* You will need to slide many times, whether you steal or not. So practice sliding until you're not afraid to "hit the dirt." The best way to do that is to "hit the grass." It's softer.

Start by practicing the drop. The faster you run, the easier it is to slide and not fall. Run hard and drop onto one side of the seat of your pants. Let your upper body fall back so that you are low as you slide toward the bag.

Now try sliding at a real base, and remember to tuck one leg under, so you can pop up on your feet.

PART TWO

IN THE FIELD

5

FIELDING GROUND BALLS

The big league infielder darts to his left. He dives. He snags the ball. He jumps to his feet, spins, and makes a perfect throw to first.

It all looks so easy.

Then your coach hits an easy grounder to you. And the stupid ball skips under your glove and between your legs.

What's going on here?

Well, remember two things. Major league players have fielded *lots* of ground balls. Thousands of them. Millions! And they have learned:

THE BIG THREE OF FIELDING GROUND BALLS

1. Keep the ball in front of you (when you can).
2. Stay low.
3. Watch the ball into your glove.

To do all that, you can't stand around with your hands on your hips. You have to be ready for the ball.

The Infielder's Stance

Just as in batting, the key to a good stance is *balance*.

1. Stand with your feet about as far apart as your shoulders.
2. Crouch, with your knees bent and your rear end low.
3. As the pitcher gets ready to throw, keep your hands or elbows on your knees.
4. As the ball is pitched, take two little steps forward and shift your weight forward, off your heels.
5. Drop your glove low, with the fingers touching (or almost touching) the ground.

Practice this stance while looking in a mirror. Try shifting your weight by taking two little steps forward.

Now you're ready. Remember the "Big Three."

Keep the Ball in Front of You (When You Can)

The ball is always easier to catch if it is in front of you. And even if you don't catch it, your body will block it and knock it down. Often, you can still make the play.

If the ball is hit to one side or the other, take one or more quick side steps and get in front of the ball.

Sometimes a ground ball will be hit so hard—or so far to your left or right—that you won't have time to get in front of it. You may have to reach and try to scoop the ball up. Or you

may have to reach across your body. That's called "back-handing." But those are tough plays.

Just make sure you don't turn an easy play into a tough one by reacting too slowly or by forgetting to move in front of the ball.

Another tough play is the slow-bouncing ball. If you wait for the ball, you will have to catch it on the bounce that happens to reach you. But if you charge the ball, you can choose the hop that's easiest to catch.

Stay Low

When an infielder misses a ground ball, the ball almost always goes *under* the glove, not over it. So remember—don't bend from the waist and stick your glove down at the last second.

If a ball is hit sharply and right at you, bend your knees and keep your rear end down. Let the fingers of your glove touch the ground. That way the ball is walled off and can-not get through.

If the ball is hit slowly, don't charge so fast that you're out of control—but don't sit back and wait, either.

Watch the Ball into Your Glove

Watch the ball from the moment it leaves the bat—and keep your eye on it.

Usually the ball will take a true bounce. If you can catch the ball on a high bounce, it is easier to field and throw. But even if it skips to the left or right or flattens out—that is, takes a bad bounce—you will be ready if you are in position and watching.

Reach forward for the ball. Don't let it get so close to your feet that you can't watch it into your glove.

Use both hands. Catch the ball with the glove, but cover it with your bare hand. Watch the ball all the way into the glove before you look up to throw.

A natural fear is that a hard-hit ball will bounce up and hit you in the face. But remember: If you watch the ball into your glove, you will usually catch it. If you look away, the ball is much more likely to bounce past your glove and hit you.

If you knock the ball down without catching it, don't look up to see where the runner is. Reach with your bare hand, get hold of the ball, and then look up to throw.

Fielding Grounders in the Outfield

All the same rules will work for outfielders. But outfielders have more time to see the ball coming, and they usually don't have to throw quite so quickly. That's why outfielders should take the time to be certain, above all, that the ball doesn't get past them.

Get all the way down on one knee to make sure you block

off any chance for the ball to get through. Be especially sure that you get in front of the ball and don't have to reach out to the side.

Remember, if a ball rolls past you in the outfield, a single might turn into a home run.

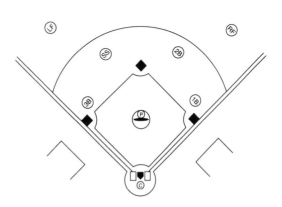

The field with players in defensive positions.

♦ ♦ ♦ ♦ PRACTICING ♦ ♦ ♦ ♦

1. *Keep the ball in front of you (when you can).*

2. *Stay low.*

Have a friend (or one of your parents) throw you a lot of slow grounders. Run to get in front of the ball—or charge it—and get into position to field it. Remember to crouch with your knees bent, your rear end low, and your glove touching the ground.

Concentrate mainly on getting in front of the ball and staying low. Have your friend call out "good position" when you do it right, even if you don't catch the ball.

3. *Watch the ball into your glove.* Have your friend throw harder and harder grounders. Practice until you feel comfortable watching the ball all the way into your glove. Ask your friend to tell you if you turn your head, or look up before the ball is in your glove.

6

CATCHING
FLY BALLS

One of the hardest skills to learn is catching a fly ball. You have to figure out where the ball will come down, run to that place, and then make the catch.

There are only three ways to learn to do that:

1. Practice. 2. **Practice. 3. PRACTICE!**

But there *are* some basic rules that will help you:

THE BIG THREE OF CATCHING FLY BALLS

1. Keep the ball in front of you (when you can).
2. Use two hands (when you can).
3. Catch the ball at eye level (when you can).

That's a lot of "when you can's." But sometimes, after a long run, you'll have to reach for the ball with one hand, or reach down low for it.

And let's face it. While you're learning, you're going to miss a lot of those tough catches.

But if you can catch the easy ones, your team is going to win a lot of games.

And, as always, that means starting from a ready stance.

The Outfielder's Stance

Sometimes things can get slow in the outfield. An inning or two might go by without a single play coming your way. But then—*bang!*—here comes the ball, and you'd better be ready.

So an outfielder has to watch the action closely, not daydream and look around.

Outfielders usually have more time to react than infielders do. So the stance of an outfielder is a little different from the infielder's.

1. Stand with your feet about as far apart as your shoulders.
2. Bend forward with your hands on your knees.
3. Watch closely so that you can pick up the ball the instant it comes off the bat.

Now remember the "Big Three."

Keep the Ball in Front of You
(When You Can)

As the ball flies off the bat, you try to guess where it will go. There is no easy way to do that. But in time you will pick up on the angle of the flight, the sound of the bat, the wind, and other clues. For now, you can only practice and keep trying.

Don't judge the flight of the ball too quickly. The worst thing you can do is charge in on a ball—that then goes over your head. So hesitate for a second, and while you keep watching the ball, run hard to the place you think it will come down. Try to get to the ball quickly, so you will have time to adjust if you have misjudged.

Some kids say, "Get under the ball." But be careful about that. You really want the ball *in front* of you. That's where you can see it best.

Use Two Hands
(When You Can)

A lot of major leaguers catch the ball with one hand. It looks easy. But don't do it—at least not while you're learning. Your glove will be much steadier if you use both hands.

If you are catching the ball above your waist—and that's where you *want* to catch it—keep your thumbs together. As the ball hits the pocket of your glove, close both hands around the ball. That will keep the ball from popping out of the glove.

Catch the Ball at Eye Level
(When You Can)

You have gotten yourself in a good position, with the ball in front of you. You have both hands up, thumbs together, fingers pointing up. Now watch the ball into your glove.

Keep your hands at eye level but out in front of your face about a foot or so. Watch the ball over the top of your glove. Then reach toward the ball as it comes to you.

Sometimes you will have to charge a low line drive. That means you have to turn your glove so the fingers are down. Still use both hands if you can. Your little fingers will be together instead of your thumbs.

Once in a while you will have to turn around and run to a ball that's hit over your head. You may have to reach high with one hand. Just do your best. It's a tough play. But the key is to keep your eye on the ball.

If you have time, run hard, then turn and face the ball and catch it with two hands. You always have a much better chance that way.

Catching Pop-ups

Not all fly balls are line drives. Often the ball pops high in the air. The first rule to remember is that if you, the outfielder, can get to the ball, you should take it.

You see the ball better than an infielder does because you are coming toward the ball.

This is one of those times when players *must* talk to each other. The outfielder should yell, ''I've got it!'' and the infielder should back off and yell, ''Take it!''

A pop-up can be hard to catch. The wind can move the ball, and the player, looking up, can lose balance very easily. So don't run too far under the ball. Keep the ball in front of you.

And use both hands!

1. *Keep the ball in front of you (when you can).*

2. *Use two hands (when you can).*

3. *Catch the ball at eye level (when you can).*

Playing catch with a friend is always good practice. You get the knack of letting your hand "give" just a little as the ball strikes the pocket of your glove. But try a game of catch in which you never reach to the side for the ball. Instead, move in front of the ball and catch it with two hands, every time.

After you have thrown the ball back and forth for a while, have your friend throw the ball high, like a rainbow. Run to get in front of the ball. Get your thumbs together and reach up and catch the ball at eye level. Keep doing that as your friend throws the ball longer and higher.

Your coach or a parent can then begin to hit flies to you. Ask for easy and fairly short ones at first, so you can learn to judge the direction and distance of the ball as it comes off the bat. But in time, practice those difficult catches. Run hard to get in front of the ball and get both hands up to eye level— *when you can!*

7
THROWING

Every player on a baseball team has to be able to throw the ball with good aim. The problem is, the worst thing you can do is . . . aim.

Okay, that may not seem to make sense.

But it does.

You may be making the short throw from second base to first. Or you may be making the long one from center field to the catcher. The rules—the "Big Three" of throwing—are still the same. And they all come down to throwing, not aiming.

THE BIG THREE OF THROWING

1. Grip the ball right.
2. Throw off your back foot.
3. Look at your target and follow through.

The "Ready" Position

When you throw a ball in a baseball game, you have either just caught it in the air or fielded it on the ground. Either way, you must make a quick, smooth motion to be ready to throw.

The instant the ball is in your glove (never *before*), you must begin to move your glove hand and your throwing hand—together—into the throwing position.

As the shoulder of your throwing arm moves back, grip the ball while it is still in your glove. And then draw back your arm, with your elbow away from your body and held high. Your body should turn so that your forward shoulder faces the target.

While your arm is moving back, hop forward once on your back foot. That's the right foot if you are right-handed, and the left foot if you are left-handed. Raise your front leg and shift your weight backward.

You are now "coiled back" and ready to throw.

That's when the "Big Three" of throwing come into play.

Grip the Ball Right

Grip the ball with your first two fingers and your thumb. Your fingers should be on top of the ball and spread apart a little. Your thumb should be under the ball. Leave a little space between your palm and the ball.

Take a firm grip, but don't squeeze too hard.

As you throw the ball, bring your arm straight over the top of your shoulder. And then, as you release the ball, snap your wrist forward and down so that the ball touches the ends of your fingers last.

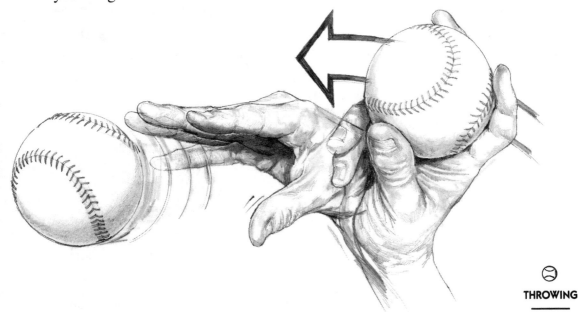

Throw off Your Back Foot

As you begin to throw, your weight must be on your back foot. As you throw, drive not only your arm but your whole body forward.

Step *directly at the target* with your front foot.

When you finish your throw, your throwing-arm shoulder should face the target.

You may think you can hurry by throwing flat-footed or with your weight forward. But your throw will either fall short or will "rainbow" and get to the target so slowly that you will lose more time than you gain.

Look at Your Target and Follow Through

When you are catching or fielding a grounder, never take your eye off the ball. But once you have the ball in your glove, never look at it.

As you grip the ball and cock your arm to throw, look at your target. Step at the target and drive your weight forward. Snap your wrist. And then continue to bring your arm through and around, completing the natural motion you have begun.

If you try to drive your hand at the target—as though you were aiming a dart—the ball will sail high. So don't aim. Just throw with a good motion while you look at the target.

Have you ever noticed that when someone says, "Hey, throw me the ball," you can throw it right to the person every time. But try to hit a target. Suddenly everything goes wrong!

That's because you are aiming, not throwing.

Some Other Ways to Throw the Ball

Sometimes you need to make your throw soft and easy. A shortstop, for instance, might be throwing to the second baseman, who is covering the bag. A hard throw would be too tough to handle. A soft, underhanded toss is best in that situation.

Sometimes you may have to get off a throw very quickly. You may have to grab a grounder and throw sidearm, for instance.

But remember, if you hurry your throw, and miss your target, you only make things worse. Sometimes you shouldn't throw at all. It's better to give up a single than to throw wildly to first and allow the runner to end up on second.

THROWING

1. *Grip the ball right.* Experiment with holding the ball with your fingers across the seams, and then with the seams. Most players find they throw best with their fingers across the seams. Now, can you dig the ball out of your glove quickly and get the grip you want?

Keep working on it!

2. *Throw off your back foot.*

3. *Look at your target and follow through.*

Play catch, but don't just throw any old way. Practice a quick, smooth motion. Grip the ball correctly. Shift your weight back and then throw with a good wrist snap and follow through.

If your coach hits fly balls to you, practice not only the catch but also the smooth motion and the strong throw back to the infield.

And pick a target. Throw to a base or to a player. Wild throws won't teach you anything.

If you take infield practice, don't just field the ball and then pat yourself on the back. Finish the play by throwing the ball to first, or to some other base.

And one warning: Don't try to throw farther or harder than your strength allows. You will get stronger as you grow older. "Overthrowing" not only produces a bad throw, it can hurt your arm.

PART THREE
POSITIONS

8
PITCHING

Pitching. That's the glory position on a baseball team.

At least it is if you win.

Pitchers have to have good arms. They also have to be able to handle pressure. The best way to do that is to learn good pitching principles. These are called—what else?—the "Big Three" of pitching.

THE BIG THREE OF PITCHING

1. Grip the ball right.
2. Use the same motion on every pitch.
3. Throw—don't aim.

Does this sound a lot like the "Big Three" of throwing? Of course it does. Pitching is fine-tuned throwing. The principles are basically the same.

Grip the Ball Right

You've heard of fastballs, curveballs, sliders, change-ups, split-fingered fastballs, knuckleballs, and maybe others.

Someday you may want to throw all of these. But let the curves and sliders wait for now. Throwing a curveball or slider at your age can be dangerous. The motion puts strain on growing muscles. Some kids have ruined their pitching arms by trying to learn to throw a curve before they were old enough.

The most important thing is to throw strikes. To do that, a good fastball, well controlled, is all you need.

Grip the ball with your first two fingers (index and middle fingers) separated a little and on top of the ball. Place your thumb under the ball. Leave a little space between the ball and the palm of your hand.

Don't grip the ball too tight. Your wrist should be loose so it will "snap" when you throw.

Use the Same Motion on Every Pitch

Learn your pitching motion and practice it until it's smooth. Your hand, wrist, arm, shoulders, back, and legs should all work together in one flowing movement.

These are the steps in a good motion:
1. Face the batter with the toes of your right foot (if you're right-handed) over the front edge of the pitching rubber. Your left foot is behind the rubber. Hold the ball behind you, so the batter can't see it.
2. Rock forward by bending at the waist. Swing your arms back toward second base. (Some players like to rock twice, just to start with a relaxed, easy feeling.)
3. As you rock backward, swing your arms up over your head. Shift your weight to your left foot. (All this time, keep the ball hidden in your glove.)
4. Turn on your right foot and push it against the front

edge of the rubber. Turn until you face third base. Your weight should shift to your right foot.

5. Pull back your throwing arm and lift your left leg at the same time. The knee of your left leg should come up to about the level of your belt.

6. Take a fairly long stride straight toward home plate. Experiment to find your natural stride. Your foot should come down flat—not on the heel or toe.

7. Get your power from pushing off and driving forward with your right leg.

8. As you throw the ball, bring your arm "over the top." Don't throw sidearm.

9. As you release with a snap of your wrist, let your arm continue in its circle. This follow-through will carry your hand past your left knee and almost to the ground.

10. Bring your right leg to the ground and face the batter. You're now an infielder, and you have to be ready.

Throw—Don't Aim

When you tell yourself, "I've *got* to throw strikes," you start to aim. And that means your motion changes. But when you use the same motion every time—without thinking about it—your body learns to throw strikes naturally.

If you "point" the ball at the strike zone, your wrist won't snap, and you won't follow through. Practice your motion until it's natural. And when you get nervous, stay with that motion.

If you can get the ball in the strike zone with good speed, you will do very well.

As you become comfortable with your ability to throw strikes, experiment with moving the ball up and down in the strike zone, and in and out. Remember, batters hit more ground balls on pitches down in the strike zone.

In time, try gripping the ball against the palm of your hand. What happens? The ball should float to the plate much slower than usual. This "change-up" can keep batters from timing your pitches too easily.

But for now, practice that smooth motion, and *follow through*. Throw. Don't aim. Let your body do what it has practiced.

♦ ♦ ♦ ♦ P R A C T I C I N G ♦ ♦ ♦ ♦

1. *Grip the ball right.* Always grip the ball the same way. But you may want to experiment with the position of the ball's seams.

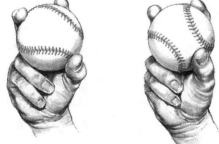

What happens when you grip the ball *across* the seams? What happens when you grip it *with* the seams? Which way gives you better control? Which way puts more movement on the ball? Control should be your first goal, but some tricky movement on the ball could be tough on the batters.

2. *Use the same motion on every pitch.*

3. *Throw—don't aim.*

Practice until your motion is part of you. If you throw to a friend, make sure the distance is the same that it will be in a game. Have the person crouch and set the target, just like a regular catcher. You may even want to set up a home plate and have a batter stand in position to give you the right feel for throwing to a strike zone.

You can also practice throwing at a target on a wall, or through a hanging tire. But when you do that, remember not to start aiming. Use your regular motion.

Always warm up before pitching. Play catch and start by throwing nice and easy. Gradually throw harder. After a hard workout, give your arm a day off. Most leagues have rules to keep you from pitching too often. Don't overwork your arm on your own.

Practice your pitching motion with your coach. Have the coach spot any problems. Maybe you're striding too long, or too short. Maybe you're not coming over the top. Maybe your grip is too tight, or you aren't snapping your wrist.

Work out the problems. When you are humming the ball over the plate, stay with that motion. Keep in mind that even the great pitchers have bad days. But if you find a good motion and then stay with it, you will do very well.

9

CATCHING

In football, the quarterback is the team leader. In baseball, the catcher leads.

Catchers are field managers. They see all the action. They signal pitches. They also call out what base to throw the ball to, and whether to cut off a throw from the outfield.

Catchers need strong arms and legs, but they also have to be smart. They have to keep track of everything.

They also need to keep the team—especially the pitcher—calm and in control.

This is no easy job!

But if you learn the ''Big Three'' of catching, you can be the quarterback of your baseball team.

THE BIG THREE OF CATCHING

1. Learn the correct catching positions.
2. Stay in front of the ball.
3. Be an infielder.

Always wear your protective gear when you practice. You need to get used to the weight and the awkward feel. Even more important, it will help keep you from getting hurt.

The ball will hit you in the chest protector or the mask. Or it will bounce off your shin guard. And you'll be fine! Your equipment will protect you. Soon you'll learn to relax behind the plate and not be scared.

Learn the Correct Catching Positions

There are two catching positions. One is for giving signals to the pitcher. The other is for catching pitches.

When you first start catching, you may not need to give signals. Your pitcher may throw only fastballs. But learn the position for the day when you need it.

The main goal of the "signal position" is to keep players on the other team from seeing your signal hand.

Crouch on the front part of your feet, with your feet quite close together and legs spread. Place your mitt against your left thigh, open, so you block the vision of the third-base coach.

Signal with your right hand against your right thigh. Most teams keep their signals simple—for example, one finger down for a fastball and two for a change-up.

Once the pitcher has the signal, you move into a "ready" position to catch the ball. Stand up and make certain you are *close enough* to the batter.

That's right.

Most kids want to get back too far. But that only makes it harder to catch a foul tip. And it gives a target that is little help to the pitcher. So stand up and reach toward the batter. Your hand should be six inches to a foot behind the hands of the batter. That's plenty of room. Remember, the batter will stride forward.

Crouch again, but this time with your feet wider apart—a little wider than your shoulders. Then sit down on an imaginary chair. Your thighs should be parallel to the ground.

Lean forward enough to get your balance and reach forward with your mitt. Set a steady target with your open glove.

Keep your bare hand against the back of your mitt, ready to help close the mitt around the ball. But hold your hand in a loose fist. This keeps fingers out of the way of foul tips.

Stay in Front of the Ball

Remember the most important rule of baseball: *Keep your eye on the ball.* Follow the ball into your glove and don't worry about what the batter does.

If the pitch is wide of the strike zone, don't reach for the ball with your arms. Instead, move your whole body. If the pitch is to your right, for instance, step with your right foot and get your body in front of the ball.

If the ball is in the dirt, drop down to your knees and get the glove down low. Don't let the ball get past you.

If the pitch is high, don't stay crouched. Stand up.

Always try to catch the ball. But if you can't catch it, block it and keep it in front of you. If the ball gets by you, you'll have to turn around and run after it. That's trouble.

Be an Infielder

If you're a catcher, you're an infielder. You throw to all the bases. You catch pop-ups. You cover a base. You field ground balls. You back up other players.

When the batter pops the ball up, let an infielder make the catch—unless you are the only one who can get to it.

If it's your catch, get your mask off quickly. But don't throw it away yet. Run to the ball. Once you have your position, throw the mask well out of your way. Get both hands up to catch the ball.

If you have to run to the screen or near the fence, you may have to take your eye off the ball for a moment. Get to where you're going, then look back up and locate the ball. Set yourself and make the catch.

When you try to tag a runner at home, move ahead of the plate a step and set yourself. Block the runner's path. Keep your eyes on the ball. Catch the ball before you try to make the tag. Then get your glove down and let the runner slide into it.

Balls hit slowly on the ground are difficult because they are bouncing away from you. Your mitt is also not as flexible as fielders' gloves. So use the glove to stop the ball and take the spin out of it. Then scoop up the ball with both hands.

When the batter hits a grounder to an infielder, and the infielder throws to first base, the catcher should run down the first-base line to help cover in case the throw gets past the first baseman. That can mean a lot of running in a game, but it will stop some runners from moving up on the bases when there's a wild throw.

At last, but *very important,* learn to make a firm and accurate throw back to the pitcher. Pitchers shouldn't have to run around to catch wild throws back to the mound. And you never want to give a runner a "gift" extra base.

♦ ♦ ♦ ♦ P R A C T I C I N G ♦ ♦ ♦ ♦

1. *Learn the correct catching positions.*
2. *Stay in front of the ball.*
3. *Be an infielder.*

You can practice your catching positions at home, but most of your practice will have to be with other players. You and a pitcher can work out together. But don't practice without your protective gear. And don't practice with a fielder's glove. Get used to that catcher's mitt.

Catch batting practice, but also be sure to take infield practice. This gives you a chance to catch infielders' throws at home, and to throw to the bases.

Watch baseball. Watch all the games you can, and think about every situation. If you're a field manager for your team, you have to know everything about the game.

You could even watch a few football games. You're the quarterback!

10

FIRST BASE

First basemen make more putouts than anyone on the team. So they have to be ready for anything. Besides the routine plays, they have to be ready to catch quick, off-balance throws. Good first basemen turn bad throws into big outs.

All that's not easy when one foot has to be on the bag. That's why good first basemen know:

```
THE BIG THREE OF PLAYING
         FIRST BASE

    1. Stretch for the throw.
    2. Keep your foot on the bag.
    3. Work with the pitcher.
```

First basemen are infielders, and they should develop the skills that every infielder needs. But they need the additional skills of the "Big Three," and that means extra practice.

First base is a position where left-handers have an advantage. Most of the throws that the first baseman makes are to the right, across the diamond, so a left-hander can field the ball and come up throwing more easily than a right-hander.

It helps, too, if the first baseman is tall. A tall player can reach for those high or wide throws, and stretch for the low ones.

Stretch for the Throw

Lots of plays at first base are close. The runner goes all out to try to beat the throw. So first basemen get an advantage by making the infielders' throws as short as possible.

They do that by reaching *toward* the ball. They stride toward the ball and reach out as far as their arms will stretch.

In youth leagues, where taking a lead is against the rules, first basemen play several steps off the bag. When the ball is hit to an infielder, they hurry to the bag and set up a target.

Young first basemen anchor the toe of their *left* foot to the inside corner of the bag (if they are left-handed) and then stretch with their *right* leg toward the ball.

With experience, first basemen learn to straddle the bag with their heels. If the throw is to their left, they hop to the left and place their right toe against the edge of the bag. Then they stretch with their left leg.

But if the ball is to their right, they hop to the right, put the toe of their left foot on the edge of the bag and stretch with their right leg.

FIRST BASE

69

But one hint to first basemen: *Never* step on the middle of the bag—unless you don't want to keep your foot. Remember that the runner is going to step there too.

Sometimes the throw is perfect and on time. That's when you hold your concentration and keep your eye on the ball. Don't stretch as far. Use both hands to catch the ball. Why take chances with one-handed catches if you don't have to?

Keep Your Foot on the Bag

Don't stretch so far that your foot comes off the base. Concentrate on pushing against the *inside corner* of the bag with your back foot.

And be sure to use your toe, not your heel. If you hold your heel against the bag, it will pull up and off the bag when you stretch.

Of course, if the ball is out of reach, try not to let it get by you. Pull your foot off the bag and go to the ball. Then try to get back to the bag if you have time.

The same goes for jumping for a high throw. Even if you miss the out, don't let the ball get by you. It's better to keep runners on first than to allow them to go to second.

Work with the Pitcher

There are two important ways that first basemen work with pitchers. In older leagues, where runners can take a lead, the first basemen must ''hold'' runners at first by playing close to the bag. Pitchers can throw to first to keep the runner close or to attempt a pickoff play. But that won't be *your* worry at first.

As a young player, you have to be ready to work with the pitcher when you are the one who fields a grounder or when the batter bunts the ball down the first-base line.

FIRST BASE

If you can field the ball and still beat the runner to the base, you should. But a good bunt or a ground ball toward second base will take you too far away from the bag.

In those situations, the pitcher should run to first base and cover the bag. The pitcher is a moving target. So toss the ball underhanded, if you have time, and lead the pitcher so that the ball is easy to grab.

♦ ♦ ♦ ♦ P R A C T I C I N G ♦ ♦ ♦ ♦

1. *Stretch for the throw.*

2. *Keep your foot on the bag.*

3. *Work with the pitcher.*

Take infield practice as often as you can. Work on all the skills you need, including throws to other bases, grounders, and bunts.

With a friend, you can work for hours at tagging the bag and stretching for throws. But don't stand in one spot and catch. Work with a bag. Stand off the bag as you would in a game. Run to the bag and get set as your friend throws to you.

Work on your stretch and your catch. Be sure you keep your toe on the bag. Practice switching feet and stretching with the leg closest to the ball.

11
INFIELD

A ground ball bounces your way. You get low and watch it right into your glove—the way you were taught.

And then what?

This is no time to start thinking about where you're going to throw the ball. You have to *know*.

Baseball can be complicated. Infielders have to make a lot of decisions. But for now, keep things simple. Just remember:

THE BIG THREE OF PLAYING THE INFIELD

1. Get an out on the lead runner (when you can).
2. Cover the right base.
3. Help outfielders relay the ball back to the infield.

You're going to make mistakes. That's part of learning.

But if you and your teammates play smart, you will stop runs that lose games.

Positioning

Get to know the hitting habits of players on opposing teams. Move up or back, left or right, according to where players tend to hit. Don't assume that all right-handed batters hit the ball to left field, though. Often, for instance, a weak right-handed hitter will hit the ball to the right side.

Your coach will show you the correct "straightaway" positions. First and third basemen usually stand even with the bag or behind it and several feet inside the foul line.

The second baseman and the shortstop share the job of covering second. They position themselves well off the bag and then shift in or out, right or left, according to the situation.

Straightaway positions.

Get an Out on the Lead Runner (When You Can)

With a runner on first and no outs (or one out), major league infielders hope for a ground ball. They want to go for a double play.

But a double play involves two quick throws and two good catches. That's not easy for young players.

Still, if you can throw to second and get the lead runner, you'll have an out and no one on second.

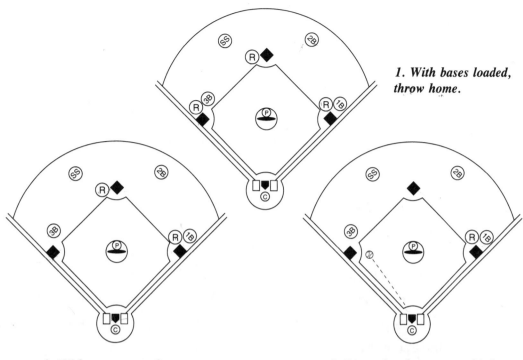

1. With bases loaded, throw home.

2. With runners on first and second, throw to third if there's time.

3. It's a slow bouncer to third. Should the infielder throw to first or second?

So go for the lead runner. With the bases loaded, throw home for the force out—if you can. With runners on first and second, throw to third for the force—if you can.

But remember, sometimes things aren't that simple.

Let's say there's a runner on first and the batter hits a slow bouncer to the third baseman. The play to second might be a good one. But a batter usually gets a slower start than the base runner. So with a fast runner on base, the play to first might be the only good one. It's better to get an out than to throw to second late and end up with *two* runners on and no one out.

In other words, an infielder has to *think ahead.* How many outs are there? How fast is the runner? How fast is the batter?

INFIELD

With two outs, your coach will yell, "Get the easy one." So you throw to the base where the throw is shortest or where the runner is least likely to beat the throw.

Cover the Right Base

It won't do a lot of good to throw to the right base if no one is there to catch the ball. Infielders have to know which base to cover on every play.

Who should cover second base—the second baseman or the shortstop? Usually, that's not too hard to know.

In most cases, if the ball is hit to the second baseman, the shortstop covers second. And if the ball is hit to the shortstop, the second baseman covers.

But supposing the second baseman makes an error on the ball and the runner tries for second? If the shortstop is standing around watching and doesn't hurry to second, the runner might make it to second when he or she could have been thrown out.

The important thing is that all bases are covered.

Let's say that a runner is on first when a batter hits a single to right field. The runner decides to go for third, and that's where everyone is looking.

The runner slides into third, but the throw beats him and he's out!

The third baseman celebrates and the shortstop goes over to give him a high-five. The second baseman yells to his friends that they just made a great play. And while all that is happening, the runner who hit the single trots over to second—and into scoring position.

BALL FIELDED BY 2nd BASEMAN— SHORTSTOP COVERS.

COVERING 2nd BASE

BALL FIELDED BY SHORTSTOP— 2nd BASEMAN COVERS.

The third baseman should always check quickly to see what the runner is doing. And the second baseman should hurry over to the bag to cover in case the runner tries to go to second.

Always keep track of whether an out is a force or not.

If the play is a force, and you receive the throw, step on the bag with your right foot (if you're right-handed) and reach with your glove toward the throw. Try to look like a first baseman.

INFIELD

But if there is no runner coming behind the one you are trying to put out, remember that *you* have to make the tag. Straddle the bag. Make the catch by watching it right into your glove.

Then put your glove down, in front of the bag, and let the runner slide into your glove. Keep your glove turned backward and, if you can, hold the ball with both hands so the runner can't knock the ball out. Pull your glove away as soon as you make the tag.

Help Outfielders Relay the Ball Back to the Infield

Sometimes outfielders can't throw the ball all the way back to the infield. When that happens, the second baseman or shortstop—whoever is closest—has to run into the shallow outfield and set a target for the outfielder. The outfielder then throws the ball to the infielder.

The infielder who catches the relay throw turns and fires the ball home, or to one of the bases.

When the shortstop goes out for the relay, the second baseman should cover second and watch to see what the runners do. He or she can then call out to the shortstop where to throw the ball.

If the second baseman takes the relay, the shortstop should cover second and let the second baseman know where to throw.

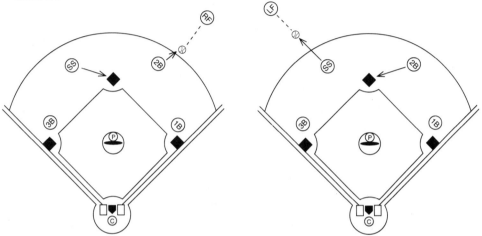

1. If the second baseman takes the relay, the shortstop covers second.

2. If the shortstop goes out for the relay, the second baseman covers second.

◆ ◆ ◆ ◆ **P R A C T I C I N G** ◆ ◆ ◆ ◆

1. *Get an out on the lead runner (when you can).*

2. *Cover the right base.*

3. *Help outfielders relay the ball back to the infield.*

Your coach will hold infield practice regularly. That will give you the chance to field grounders and throw to first or to another base, or to come home with the ball. The coach should also have you work on double-play relays, and on fielding bunts—all the things that might happen in a game.

INFIELD

At home, or with a friend, you can work on fielding ground balls, catching pop-ups, and making quick, accurate throws.

You can also set up special situations. Pretend you are covering second base, for example, from the shortstop position. Run to a spot and have your friend throw the ball to you. Step on the bag and then relay the ball back.

The more time you spend getting comfortable and confident with all the infield skills, the better you will play. So try every situation: tagging out a sliding runner; tagging a runner in a rundown; grabbing a slow-bouncing ball and going to second with the throw. What other skills can you think of?

12

OUTFIELD

The outfield is great. Nothing much happens out there. You can stay around and watch the clouds float by.

Right?

No way!

If you play the outfield the way you should, you'll be ready to run at any second—and you'll run plenty.

THE BIG THREE OF PLAYING THE OUTFIELD

1. Use your head.
2. Back up other players.
3. Talk to your teammates.

The outfield can seem slow at times. But then suddenly you have to move, and move fast. And not only that. You usually have to make decisions on every play. So you not only have to move fast, you have to *think* fast.

Use Your Head

Outfielders should be fast runners. But if you run fast in the wrong direction, your speed will only get you in trouble. Above all, outfielders have to think and *judge*.

You're charging a sinking line drive. Should you dive for it? If it gets by you, it may roll a long way, and a single will turn into an extra-base hit.

That's why you have to think about your situation *ahead of time*. Maybe the score is tied in the bottom of the last inning and a runner is in scoring position. In that situation, you have to gamble and dive for the ball. You have nothing to lose.

But if you're ahead by three runs, it's better to let one run score and hold the batter to a single.

So know the score, the number of outs, and where the runners are. And think about all the things that might happen.

In most cases, you should throw the ball to the base ahead of the lead runner. On a long hit, look for your cutoff infielder.

Before each play, think about what you'll do if the ball comes to you. For example, you might think, "If a ground ball gets through the infield, I'm throwing home." Or, "If I catch a fly ball, I'll throw to second to keep the runner on first from moving up a base."

The more you play, the more you will know what to do. But the best players never stop thinking.

Back Up Other Players

On every play—except a walk—you should be moving somewhere. And more often than not, you will be running hard.

Suppose you're playing left field. The ball is hit right at the shortstop. You say, "Good. That's a sure out." You stand there and count your lucky stars that the ball wasn't a long fly.

And then the ball rolls between the shortstop's legs!

He turns around and runs after it, and you take off, hard, trying to get there first. By the time you reach the ball, the runner is standing on second—laughing.

Sure, the shortstop made the error. But *you're* the one who let the runner get to second. Back up those infielders!

The same goes for backing up the other outfielders. You don't say, "Good, that's to the center fielder, not to me." You run toward the ball, but behind the center fielder. If the

OUTFIELD

center fielder doesn't make the catch, you're there to stop the ball from getting away.

Here's a situation to think about: No outs. A runner on first. The batter hits a hard grounder to third base.

What does the left fielder do?

That's right. The left fielder *backs up* the third baseman, in case the ball should get through.

So the other two outfielders don't have to do anything, right?

Wrong!

The third baseman has to make the long throw to first—and that can be tough. So the right fielder runs down the foul line to back up the first baseman.

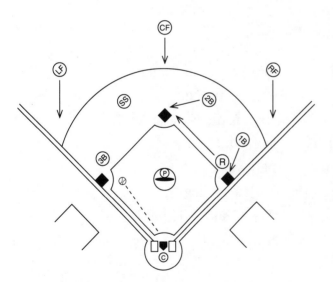

Or wait a minute. Maybe that's not what the third baseman decides to do. What if the third baseman decides to try to throw out the lead runner at second? The ball could get by the second baseman—and so the center fielder is there, backing up second.

Everyone plays smart—they don't give *anything* away.

Backup positions for fielders when a ground ball is hit to third and a man is on first.

Talk to Your Teammates

Good players communicate.

Before a play everyone holds up a fist, or one or two fingers (like horns, so you can see the fingers), and yells out the number of outs.

The coach may yell, "The play's at home!" Or during a play the coach might shout, "The runner's tagging. Throw to second!"

(2 OUTS)

But the most important time to "talk to each other" is when two or more players are chasing the same ball.

Let's say the ball is popped up on the left side. The shortstop and third baseman both go for it, and so does the left fielder.

Who takes it?

OUTFIELD

Remember, the outfielders are running in, so they have the easiest play. If the left fielder can get to the ball, he or she should shout, *loudly,* "I've got it!"

And the infielders should answer, "Take it!"

What if both an infielder and an outfielder call for it?

Remember, it's the outfielder's play. So the infielder should back off and shout, "Take it!"

But this should never happen at the last second.

So yell early and loud and keep yelling. Make sure the decision is made while the ball is still high in the air.

♦ ♦ ♦ ♦ P R A C T I C I N G ♦ ♦ ♦ ♦

1. *Use your head.*

2. *Back up other players.*

3. *Talk to your teammates.*

The only way to master all these skills is to play the game. So it's important, at practice, for your coach to set up game situations. It's also very useful to play practice games.

But there are also things you can do on your own.

When your coach is hitting fly balls to you in the outfield, practice calling for the ball, catching it, and making a smooth, strong throw to a target. And if you see the ball in flight and someone else calling for it, move over and back the player up.

Above all, *think* baseball. Watch games—from Little League to major league—and ask yourself, "If I were playing center field, what would I do in this situation?"

You have to practice to be a good baseball player. But the great players do more than play well. They *think* good baseball.

PART FOUR

ATTITUDE

13

TEAMWORK

Baseball is a team sport.

It's fun to hit a home run or make a great defensive play. But the team that learns to play as a unit will enjoy the game the most—and will win the most games.

THE BIG THREE FOR PLAYING AS A TEAM

1. Listen to your coach.
2. Support your teammates.
3. Be a good sport.

Listen to Your Coach

You're just learning the game. But that's not so bad. Knowing that you still have a lot to learn might be the best thing you have going for you. Who wants cocky players who think they already know everything?

Listen to your coach and learn. Some kids with a lot of talent never become first-rate players simply because they won't take advice.

Maybe you have your heart set on playing shortstop. And then the coach puts you in center field.

What should you do?

Be the best center fielder you know how to be! And that means you work to learn your position, and you play hard in every game. Let the coach decide how the team fits together.

Support Your Teammates

The bases are loaded. The game is on the line. And who comes up to bat? The worst hitter on the team.

He strikes out, and you're mad.

You kick the fence and say, "Why can't that stupid kid learn to hit?"

But remember, that "stupid kid" wanted more than anything to get a hit. Maybe he tried *too* hard.

The more pressure you put on a player who makes mistakes, the worse that player will play. You can depend on it. And how will you feel if *you* mess up?

On a good team, players don't have to worry about their teammates putting them down. When someone makes a mistake, the others say, "That's all right. We'll get those guys."

What about those days when everything goes *right?* After the game, do you add up all your statistics and then brag about your batting average or how many home runs you've hit?

There's nothing wrong with taking pride in your own success. But remember, you are playing on a team, and the only stat that really counts is the team victory.

Be a Good Sport

Some kids think they have to "ride" the players on other teams. But not the best players. They play hard and they enjoy winning, but they don't put the other team down.

When the game is over, win or lose, they line up and congratulate the players on the other team.

Some players are bad sports in another way. They lose their temper not only at others but at themselves. They throw their bats or batting helmets when they strike out. Or they walk around mumbling and kicking up dirt after they make a bad play in the field.

But when players get angry, they are almost sure to do worse, not better. To play well, a player needs to be relaxed and confident—not angry.

Some players worry too much about winning every game. They feel they can't enjoy baseball unless they win. But remember, even the best teams lose games—many of them. Other players don't really try hard enough. They let their team down by giving only half an effort.

The best players go hard all the time. They treat everyone, on both teams, with respect. And they have a great time!

♦ ♦ ♦ ♦ P R A C T I C I N G ♦ ♦ ♦ ♦

1. *Listen to your coach.*

2. *Support your teammates.*

3. *Be a good sport.*

At your next game, watch for a chance to tell players what they did *right*. When any player makes a good play, say something about it.

Watch for the little things: the player who hustles, who backs up a play, or who runs hard on the bases. Go out of your way to congratulate players who do something well—especially if they are struggling to learn the game.

TEAMWORK

One last reminder. Baseball is a game.

The best ballplayers love the competition and the excitement. They get fired up, and they go all out.

But they never forget to have fun!

SOME BASEBALL
WORDS AND PHRASES

Base coach A team member or coach who helps direct base runners. One coach stands near first base and another near third base.

Base on balls *See* Walk.

Batter's box The marked-off area in which a batter must stand while batting.

Bunt An intentionally soft hit that is the result of the batter allowing the ball to strike the bat and that rolls only a short distance.

Change-up An intentionally slow pitch meant to throw off a batter's timing.

Charge the ball To run toward a ground ball rather than to wait for it.

Count The number of balls and strikes called on a batter.

Cutoff The act of cutting off a throw from an outfielder.

Defensive player A member of the team that is not batting.

Double play A play that results in two outs.

Error A fielding mistake that allows a batter to reach base or a runner to advance additional base(s).

Fair ball A ball hit in fair territory—that is, within the foul lines.

Follow-through The continuation of a motion when batting or throwing.

Force, force-out An out resulting from a defensive player touching a base while holding the ball. The base runner must have no option of returning to the previously tagged base.

Foul ball A hit ball that lands in foul territory—that is, outside the foul lines.

Foul tip A foul ball that barely touches the bat and doesn't rise above the catcher's head.

Ground ball, grounder A hit ball that bounces or rolls on the grass or ground.

Infield The area of a baseball field in which the pitcher, first baseman, second baseman, shortstop, and third baseman stand.

Inning A turn at bat and a turn in the field for both teams.

Lead runner The first runner when more than one are on base.

Line drive A hard-hit ball that stays low and parallel to the ground.

Mound The raised part of the infield where the pitcher stands.

Outfield The area where the left fielder, center fielder, and right fielder stand.

thrown ball that cannot be
fielder for whom it is in-

k throw that attempts to
catch a runner off base.

Pocket The part of a glove shaped to catch the baseball.

Pop-up, pop fly A hit ball that flies high in the air.

Pop-up slide A style of slide that allows the runner to tag the base and rise quickly to his or her feet.

Pulling the ball The action of hitting the ball to left field when batting right-handed, or to right field when batting left-handed.

Putout Any play that results in an out for the opposing team.

Rounding Intentionally running past a base, prepared to continue on to the next base.

Rundown The attempt to tag out a runner who is caught between bases.

Sacrifice bunt A bunt that results in the batter being out but that advances a runner to another base.

Setting the target The catcher's positioning of the glove so that the pitcher sees where the ball should be pitched.

Slide Dropping to the ground and skidding to a base in order to avoid a tag.

Snap the ball Flipping the wrist quickly as the ball is thrown to increase the speed and accuracy of the throw.

Stealing A runner advancing to another base while the pitcher makes a pitch.

Straightaway Playing a defensive position in the normal spot.

Stride The step taken with the front foot as a batter is about to swing.

Strike zone The area directly above home plate that is between a batter's knees and chest.

Tag A term used in two ways: (1) the act of a runner stepping on a base; (2) the act of a defensive player touching a runner with the ball.

Tagging up Staying at a base (or returning to it) after a fly ball is hit, and then running to the next base after the fielder catches the ball.

Taking a lead A runner's attempt to get closer to the next base by advancing a few steps away from the base where he or she is standing.

Walk When a batter draws four pitches outside the strike zone during his or her turn at bat and goes to first.

INDEX